NATIONAL PARKS

YELLOWSTONE
NATIONAL PARK

by Cecilia Pinto McCarthy

Content Consultant
Jim Halfpenny, PhD
Scientist and Educator, A Naturalist's World

Core Library

An Imprint of Abdo Publishing
abdopublishing.com

abdopublishing.com

Published by Abdo Publishing, a division of ABDO, PO Box 398166, Minneapolis, Minnesota 55439. Copyright © 2017 by Abdo Consulting Group, Inc. International copyrights reserved in all countries. No part of this book may be reproduced in any form without written permission from the publisher. Core Library™ is a trademark and logo of Abdo Publishing.

Printed in the United States of America, North Mankato, Minnesota
072016
012017

Cover Photo: Shutterstock Images
Interior Photos: Shutterstock Images, 1, 7, 18, 45; Jim Peaco/Yellowstone National Park, 4; Diane Renkin/Yellowstone National Park, 10, 25; Agil Leonardo/Shutterstock Images, 15; Jay Fleming/Yellowstone National Park, 21; Red Line Editorial, 23; Douglas C. Pizac/AP Images, 28; William Henry Jackson, 32; Neal Herbert/Yellowstone National Park, 34; Mike Lewelling/National Park Service, 40; National Park Service, 42–43

Editor: Mirella Miller
Series Designer: Ryan Gale

Publisher's Cataloging-in-Publication Data

Names: McCarthy, Cecilia Pinto, author.
Title: Yellowstone National Park / by Cecilia Pinto McCarthy.
Description: Minneapolis, MN : Abdo Publishing, 2017. | Series: National parks
    | Includes bibliographical references and index.
Identifiers: LCCN 2016945460 | ISBN 9781680784756 (lib. bdg.) |
    ISBN 9781680798609 (ebook)
Subjects: LCSH: Yellowstone National Park--Juvenile literature.
Classification: DDC 917.87/52--dc23
LC record available at http://lccn.loc.gov/2016945460

CHAPTER ONE

THE WORLD'S FIRST NATIONAL PARK

Snow covers Yellowstone National Park in early November. The deep snow does not stop a pack of wolves. They tear hungrily at an elk carcass. Two wolves wear radio collars. Biologists put the collars on the wolves to track them. Signals from the collars have led them to the kill site. The researchers watch the animals and take notes. The data they collect will help them better understand

Nothing goes to waste in Yellowstone's rugged wilderness.

Getting to Yellowstone National Park was difficult for most of the 1800s. The nearest railroad stopped 500 miles (805 km) from the park. Visitors then had to ride a stagecoach the rest of the way. Only 300 people visited Yellowstone in 1872, its first year as a national park. Attendance began to soar after completion of the Northern Pacific Railway in 1883. Now more than 4 million people from around the world visit the park each year.

the role of wolves in the park ecosystem. The wolves eventually leave the carcass. Ravens and a coyote take their place.

Yellowstone National Park is known for its wildlife. Wolves, coyotes, elk, and ravens are a few of the almost 400 species that live there. The park is also known for its geysers, waterfalls, hot springs, and forests.

Most of Yellowstone is located in northwest Wyoming. The park also spreads into Idaho and Montana. Mountain ranges border all sides of Yellowstone, which gets its name from the Yellowstone River. The river runs through the park.

The Yellowstone River is the longest river without a dam in the lower 48 states.

A Land of Extremes

The weather in Yellowstone can be unpredictable. Winter temperatures drop below freezing. The average yearly snowfall is approximately 150 inches (381 cm). Heavy snowstorms and avalanches occur in both winter and spring. Summer brings booming afternoon thunderstorms.

The animals in Yellowstone adapt to the extreme climate. They also adapt to different habitats. There are forests, meadows, and grasslands. Rivers, streams, and lakes provide fish for grizzly bears, eagles, and other wildlife.

The park's best-known attractions are its volcanic features. Magma and heat come to the earth's surface and melt rock. The rocks warm the groundwater. Mud bubbles from the ground in some areas. Water and steam also explode into the air.

Yellowstone's unusual natural features amazed early explorers. They believed the land should be set aside for tourism. On March 1, 1872, Yellowstone became the first national park in the world.

Businessman and explorer Nathaniel P. Langford was a member of the 1870 trip that explored the Yellowstone area. In this excerpt from *Scribner's Monthly*, Langford describes the scene from a mountaintop in Yellowstone:

> *The lake and valley surrounding it lay seemingly at our feet within jumping distance. Beyond them we saw with great distinctness the jets of the mud volcano and geyser. But beyond all these, stretching way into a horizon of cloud-defined mountains, was the entire Wind River range. . . . Outside of these, on either border, along the entire range, lofty peaks rose at intervals, seemingly vying with each other in the varied splendors they presented to the beholder. The scene was full of majesty. The valley . . . was dotted with small lakes and cloven centrally by the river.*

Source: Nathaniel Pitt Langford. The Wonders of the Yellowstone. *Scribner's Monthly*, Vol. II. New York, June 1871. Google Book Search. Web. Accessed May 18, 2016.

Consider Your Audience

Consider how you would adapt this passage for a different audience, such as your parents or friends. Write a blog post conveying this same information for the new audience. How does your post differ from the original text and why?

THE GEOLOGY OF YELLOWSTONE

Yellowstone National Park is always changing. Glaciers and volcanoes formed the landscape millions of years ago. Glaciers are thick masses of ice. They form when snow is packed down over a long period of time. Glaciers flow down mountainsides. But they travel extremely slowly. Glaciers melt as climates warm.

Glaciers carved out valleys and dug out lakes in Yellowstone National Park.

Glaciers once covered Yellowstone. The glaciers shaped jagged mountain peaks. Glaciers also picked up rocks as they moved over the land. The rocks and rubble left behind after the glaciers melted formed ridges called moraines. Some rocks were massive boulders. They weigh hundreds of tons. These boulders are scattered across Yellowstone. Today, Yellowstone's landscape is lush and green. It is hard to believe the land was once covered by ice.

Volcanoes Past and Present

Glaciers added to Yellowstone's terrain. But the area's volcanic activity has also played a major role. Yellowstone National Park is one of the world's most active volcanic regions. Yellowstone sits on top of a volcanic hotspot. A hotspot forms below the earth's surface. Extreme heat comes from the planet's outer core. The heat travels upward. It then heats solid rock. The heat and hot rock continue to rise upward. They melt nearby rock into magma. A large area in the lower crust contains magma. This spreads into a chamber beneath Yellowstone's surface. This magma seeps through cracks to form the Yellowstone volcano.

Three volcanic eruptions formed Yellowstone. The eruptions happened during the last 2.1 million years. Large amounts of magma and explosive gases collected in chambers below Earth's crust. The magma and gases caused enormous pressure and stress. This led to earthquakes and eruptions. Each volcanic event sent magma, ash, gas, and rock bursting into the air for miles. The roofs of the chambers collapsed after each eruption. The collapses formed

PERSPECTIVES
Will Yellowstone Erupt?

Many people think Yellowstone is due for a super eruption. A super eruption is an enormous eruption that deposits at least 240 cubic miles (1,000 cubic km) of molten material. Dr. Jacob Lowenstern is a research geologist with the Yellowstone Volcano Observatory.

Along with other scientists, Lowenstern monitors Yellowstone's volcanic activity. He believes Yellowstone may erupt in the future. But he says not to expect a super eruption for at least a few centuries.

craters called calderas. The most recent eruption was 640,000 years ago. It formed the Yellowstone Caldera. The Caldera is 35 miles (56 km) wide and 55 miles (88 km) long.

Yellowstone's rocks are signs of its volcanic history. Rocks made by lava flows cover the park. Mesa Falls and Lava Creek Tuff are two Yellowstone landmarks made of flattened hard lava. Another volcanic natural wonder is Obsidian Cliff. The cliff is made of obsidian, a smooth volcanic glass. It forms when magma cools rapidly. American Indians made obsidian into knives, as well as spear and arrow tips.

In Hot Water

More than 10,000 hydrothermal wonders are located in Yellowstone. These include hot springs, geysers, fumaroles, and mud pots. Hydrothermal features form when snow and rain seep into the ground. Then hot rocks heat the water and create pressure. The hot water is forced upward, releasing the pressure.

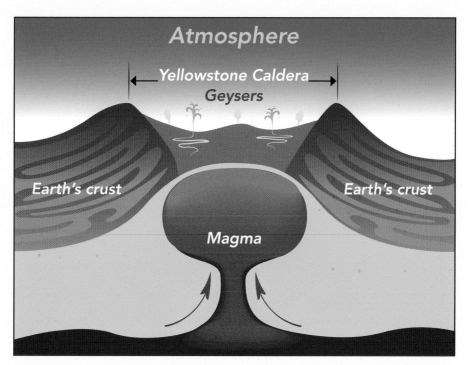

The Yellowstone Caldera

The diagram shows the Yellowstone Caldera and the activity beneath it. Where does groundwater collect? How is the water heated? What other activity does the volcano trigger?

Hot springs are the most common hydrothermal features at Yellowstone. They form when heated groundwater rises and forms pools. Currents move the water around. This action keeps the temperature lower around the pool's edges. Many different types of colorful bacteria live in hot springs. Some live in hot parts of the pool. Others thrive only in the cooler water along the edge. Yellowstone's largest hot spring

Heat-Loving Microbes

Yellowstone's hot springs are harsh places to live. Water temperatures are hot. Also much of the water is acidic and toxic. Scientists believe these extreme conditions mimic what Earth was like billions of years ago. They study how Yellowstone's microbes survive. This helps biologists better understand the limits needed for life to exist. Such studies might also reveal how life on Earth started and evolved. Microbes may hold the key to understanding if life can exist on other planets with extreme conditions.

is the rainbow-colored Grand Prismatic Spring.

Yellowstone has close to 500 geysers. This is more than anywhere else on Earth. Geysers form when hot groundwater flows through tight spaces in underground cracks. The hot water is under high pressure. It boils and steams. Then the water erupts with great force. Yellowstone's most famous geyser is Old Faithful. It was named because it dependably erupts approximately every 90 minutes.

The hottest hydrothermal features are fumaroles, or steam vents. These openings contain small amounts of water that quickly evaporate into hot steam. Fumaroles give off both steam and other gases. This makes loud hissing sounds.

Mud pots are similar to fumaroles. But mud pots do not have much water. They form when water collects in shallow clay-lined dips in the ground. The water is heated by steam rising from underneath. Mud pots often give off hydrogen sulfide gas. The gas stinks like rotten eggs. Microbes living in the water change the gas to sulfuric acid. The acid dissolves rock, creating a muddy pool. Gases bubble up through the mud.

EXPLORE ONLINE

Chapter Two discusses volcanic activity at Yellowstone. Go to the website listed below and read the article. As you know, every source is different. What new information did you learn from the article? How is the information from the website similar to the information in Chapter Two?

Distant Quake Changes Geyser Eruptions

mycorelibrary.com/yellowstone

ANIMALS AND PLANTS OF YELLOWSTONE

Yellowstone National Park is part of the Greater Yellowstone Ecosystem. This ecosystem supports several types of habitats. Alpine tundra is a rocky, treeless mountaintop location. Lush meadows are filled with wildflowers and shrubs. The sage-steppe grasslands are flat, treeless areas. They are hot and dry during the summer. They are cold and gusty in the winter.

American bison herds can be seen in Yellowstone's Hayden and Lamar Valleys.

Yellowstone's habitats are home to approximately 60 different mammal species. These mammals include grizzly bears, wolves, mountain lions, bats, and mice. Other mammals include bison, bighorn sheep, and elk. Herds of bison and elk number in the thousands. Many of them migrate within and outside of the park.

Since 1872, 285 species of birds have been recorded in Yellowstone. Of these, 150 species nest in the park. Ongoing studies track the well-being of bald eagles. The common loon, songbirds, and woodpeckers are also tracked.

Amphibian species also live in the park. They include the blotched tiger salamander, two types of frogs, and the boreal toad. Five species of snakes and the sagebrush lizard can also be found. Scientists closely monitor these populations. They are sensitive to diseases and climate changes. Shifts up or down in animal populations indicate possible problems.

Most Yellowstone streams and lakes did not have fish when the park opened in 1872. In 1889

Cutthroat trout are being reintroduced into Yellowstone's lakes and rivers.

park managers brought in fish. They wanted to make fishing easy for visitors. Stocking lakes with outside fish created serious problems. The native Arctic grayling population decreased. So did the cutthroat trout population. There is a plan, however, to restore the park's native fish species.

Managing Wolves and Bison

Managing mammals within Yellowstone is a challenge. Wolf and bison numbers have changed drastically throughout the years. Wolves were always part of Yellowstone. But in the late 1800s and early 1900s, they were seen as a threat. People considered the predators a danger to people and other animals. Landowners, farmers, hunters, and the US government tried to eliminate all wolves. Even park rangers killed wolves. In 1926 the last of Yellowstone's wolves was killed.

Research has since showed that predators help keep ecosystems healthy. Biologists studied how wolves affected the populations of other animals and plants. A plan was made to reintroduce wolves into Yellowstone. In 1995 and 1996, 31 gray wolves from Canada were released into the park. Scientists have monitored the wolves. By December 2014 approximately 100 wolves lived within Yellowstone.

Wild bison populations in Yellowstone have also changed over the years. An estimated 30 to 60 million lived in North America before the mid-1800s. Then European Americans settled in the West. They killed bison for their hides, meat, and bones. Homes and farms replaced bison grazing land. By 1889 only

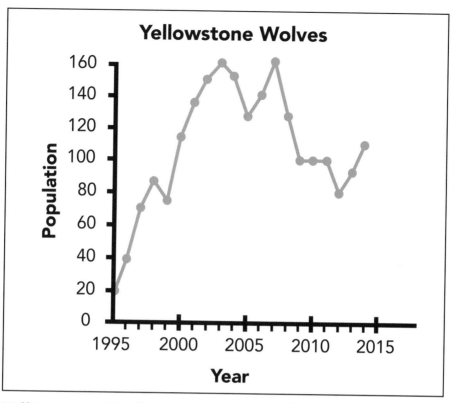

Yellowstone Wolves

Yellowstone Wolf Population
The graph shows how Yellowstone's wolf population
has changed over the years. Why do you think the wolf
population decreased? What things can happen for the wolf
population to grow again?

1,091 wild bison remained. By 1902 approximately

25 bison lived in Yellowstone. Now Yellowstone boasts

the largest population of wild plains bison. Thanks to

conservation efforts, approximately 5,000 bison live in

the park.

Protecting Grizzlies

Yellowstone is known for its grizzly bears. Since 1975 the bears have been on an endangered wildlife list. Protection of the grizzlies has been successful, though. Their numbers have increased. Now the US Fish and Wildlife Service wants to remove grizzlies from the list. This means the federal government will no longer protect them. Wildlife biologist David Mattson thinks it is too early to take grizzlies off the list. He notes that whitebark pine trees are diminishing. Nuts from these trees are a major food source for grizzlies. Without the nuts grizzlies may need to travel further to find food.

Plant Life

Yellowstone's varied landscape and weather conditions produce a wide range of plant life. The park contains wet meadows and dry shrublands. Approximately 80 percent of the park is forest. Lodgepole pines are common. These trees can reach 75 feet (23 m) in height. They grow best in open, sunny areas. But they can also handle extreme wetness and poor soil. Lodgepoles can grow where other species of trees cannot survive. There is also whitebark

More than 1,000 native species of plants thrive in Yellowstone.

Beneficial Fire

Fire is vital to Yellowstone's ecosystem. Fires have burned at Yellowstone for thousands of years. But in the summer of 1988, a massive fire affected approximately one-third of the park. Many people believed Yellowstone had been destroyed. But fire leads to new growth. Lodgepole pine trees need fire to spread their seeds. The fire's heat pops open Lodgepole pinecones. The seeds fall to the ground. Then they grow into new plants. Ashes created by fires fertilize the soil. When large trees burn down, wildflowers grow in the newly open sunny plots. Elk eat burned tree bark. Woodpeckers nest in the standing dead trees.

pine and Douglas fir. Spruce, quaking aspen, and cottonwood also cover the land.

Three species of plants are unique to Yellowstone. They do not grow anywhere else in the world. Ross's bent grass grows in two geyser basins. This flowering plant prefers the warm soil temperatures near steam vents. It grows quickly and dies off by July each year.

Another rare plant is Yellowstone sand verbena. The low-growing wildflower once grew in several areas of the park.

Erosion and trampling by visitors and animals affected the plant's population. Now it is only found along the shore of Yellowstone Lake. Yellowstone sulfur buckwheat is also only found in Yellowstone National Park. This species of buckwheat can live in dry, infertile areas. It grows near the park's geysers.

FURTHER EVIDENCE

Chapter Three has quite a bit of information about the animals and plants in Yellowstone National Park. Review the chapter and identify its main point. What key evidence supports this point? Go to the website below and explore more ideas about biodiversity. Find a quote from the website that supports the chapter's main point.

Biodiversity in Yellowstone

mycorelibrary.com/yellowstone

CHAPTER FOUR

HUMANS IN YELLOWSTONE

Archeologists believe people began living in the Yellowstone area around 11,000 years ago. They doubt people lived there when glaciers covered the area. But the glaciers started melting approximately 15,000 years ago. Stone tools found in Yellowstone show that these early humans hunted. They also searched for berries, seeds, and other plant foods. Researchers know of more than 1,800 sites with

American Indians still celebrate their cultures' traditions near Yellowstone.

evidence that humans lived in Yellowstone long ago.

Several American Indian nations made the Yellowstone region their home for thousands of years. These include the Crow and Shoshone. One group of Shoshone, the Sheepeaters, lived in Yellowstone's mountains. They got their name from the bighorn sheep they hunted. Trails through Yellowstone show where groups traveled to use resources. American Indians hunted animals, fished, and ate plants.

They used the hot springs and geysers for healing and religious ceremonies.

Europeans Come to Yellowstone

The Yellowstone area is remote. Few European settlers traveled there. The first Europeans to explore Yellowstone were fur traders. They arrived in the early 1800s. They returned to their home states with stories of boiling mud pots and jets of hot water and steam. Most people did not believe them.

In 1869 surveyor David E. Folsom set out to explore the Yellowstone region. Charles W. Cook and William Peterson accompanied him. Folsom wrote an article about the expedition when he returned. Publishers refused to print it. They believed it was fiction. Folsom, Cook, and Peterson inspired a second set of explorers. The group contained several important men, including Surveyor-General Henry D. Washburn, businessman Nathaniel P. Langford, and attorney Cornelius Hedges. They closely examined many of Yellowstone's features. Langford wrote about

William Henry Jackson captured an image of Lower Falls in 1871.

his trek. He also gave lectures about Yellowstone. Huge crowds came to hear him speak.

A third group set out for Yellowstone in 1871. Led by Ferdinand V. Hayden, this team included several scientists. They collected more information than ever before. They gathered data on Yellowstone's birds, plants, and geologic features. Artists Thomas Moran and Henry W. Elliott and photographer William Henry Jackson spent days recording the landscape. Their work gave Americans their first glimpse of Yellowstone's beauty.

Explorers lobbied Congress to protect the area. Support came from businessmen building the Northern Pacific Railway. They wanted to build the railroad out to Yellowstone. Then they could make money from tourists. The lobbying worked. On March 1, 1872, President Ulysses S. Grant signed the bill. Yellowstone National Park was born.

Managing Yellowstone

President Grant signed a bill making Yellowstone a national park. But Congress set aside little money to protect or manage the park. There were only a few visitors at first. They did a great deal of damage. They cut off chunks of geysers and other formations as souvenirs. Hunters killed huge numbers of elk and other animals. Companies were allowed to lease parts of the park. They cut trees, killed animals, and farmed on the land. US Army General Philip Sheridan was shocked by the destruction. In 1886 he sent troops to take control of Yellowstone. The US Army stayed to manage Yellowstone for 30 years. In 1916 the National Park Service was created to oversee national parks.

YELLOWSTONE TODAY

Yellowstone National Park continues to grow in popularity. Attendance reached an all-time high in 2015. More than 4 million tourists visited. Most visitors come between May and September.

There are many ways to enjoy Yellowstone. Visitors can tour by bus. Or they can drive themselves. A 310-mile (500-km) network of paved roads winds through the park. Driving the Grand Loop road is one

Visitors gather to watch a steaming geyser.

of the best ways. This figure eight–shaped roadway passes by many popular spots. The loop passes by Old Faithful, Yellowstone Lake, and Mammoth Hot Springs. Backcountry trails and thousands of campsites may appeal to more adventurous travelers. Herds of elk and bison wander the meadows of the Madison and West Yellowstone areas. Grizzly bears and wolves are more common in Hayden Valley, Lamar Valley, and Mount Washburn. Visitors can fish, bike, boat, and ride horses. Even in winter there is still plenty to do. Snowshoeing, cross-country skiing, and snowmobiling are popular winter activities. Lodging options include the historic Old Faithful Inn, hotels, cabins, tents, and RV parks.

The National Park Service

The creation of Yellowstone National Park led to other national parks and monuments. In 1916 President Woodrow Wilson created the National Park Service (NPS). This organization oversees the management of more than 400 federal parks, monuments, and reservations. The NPS has more than 780 summer employees working at Yellowstone. Rangers and educators interact with visitors. They also teach programs. Other employees make sure the trails, roads, and buildings are well maintained and safe.

A Hotbed of Research

Yellowstone is ideal for study. Its biodiversity, archeological treasures, and geologic features make it unique. Each year up to 200 scientists receive permits to do

PERSPECTIVES

Cell Phones in Yellowstone

In 2013 the NPS approved a plan to build a cell tower in Yellowstone. The park already has five towers. These towers provide service to more than 50 percent of the park. But park managers feel expanded and better cell phone service will help keep visitors safe. It allows rangers and visitors to talk in case of an emergency. Not everyone agrees, however. A group called Public Employees for Environmental Responsibility opposes expanded cell phone service. They believe cell phones do not belong in national parks. They argue that cell phone noise will ruin other visitors' experiences.

Climate Change

Scientists track climate changes at Yellowstone. They have done this for 50 years. Average temperatures have increased during the 50 years of tracking. Scientists have recorded more days per year above freezing. Fewer days with snow on the ground have also been recorded. These changes affect the park's plants and animals. A change in snowmelt affects water levels and plant growth. It also changes bison migration and fish reproduction. It even affects when insects arrive. Park scientists are trying to predict how climate change will affect the park in the future.

research projects in Yellowstone. One project is the Yellowstone Wolf Project. Since 1995 scientists have followed generations of wolves. Some wolves wear global positioning system (GPS) collars. Their activity is monitored, and data is collected. Researchers learn how wolves survive, interact with each other, and affect other animals.

University researchers study Yellowstone's ancient cultures. Artifacts show that early people were both hunters and gatherers. Clues left behind include arrow and spear points, stone knives, and hearths used for cooking and heating.

Protecting the Park

Yellowstone must deal with several ongoing challenges. Natural fires are a normal and necessary part of the ecosystem. Fire gets rid of debris. It also replenishes nutrients and encourages the regrowth of plants. But people living near the park worry that massive fires are a hazard. Yellowstone authorities try to strike a balance. They manage fires to protect the public. They also allow managed fires to benefit the local ecology.

Wildlife must also be managed. Bison migrate outside of Yellowstone in search of food in winter months. They sometimes roam into developed areas. Ranchers worry that migrating bison may spread disease. Bison also graze in areas reserved for cattle. Some bison are infected with a disease dangerous to cattle.

Yellowstone employees are well trained on dealing with wildfires.

Yellowstone's increasing popularity raises questions about how best to protect the park. Millions come to enjoy Yellowstone's natural beauty. But increased tourism also means more litter, air pollution, and water pollution. Cars, planes, and snowmobiles add pollution, traffic jams, and noise. Too many visitors also disrupt wildlife.

A balance must be struck between enjoying Yellowstone while preserving its wildlife and natural features. Cooperation between the government and citizens is necessary. Only then can Yellowstone's natural treasures be preserved.

Journalist John Lancaster examined the conflict between development and maintaining the wildness of Yellowstone in a *Washington Post* article. He wrote:

> *One is the Yellowstone . . . where a visitor can wander through a landscape little changed since . . . 1807.*
>
> *The other is the recreational Yellowstone, where the same visitor can rent a motorboat or a snowmobile, rough it in a $95-a-night hotel and soak up many . . . sights without ever setting foot outside a car. . . .*
>
> *Environmentalists argue that in a rapidly developing world, the 50 national parks can play a vital role as reservoirs of biological diversity. And they are critical of the private concessionaires that run hotels, stores and restaurants within the parks . . .*

Source: "Tourist Mecca or Home for Nature: Two Visions of Yellowstone." Washington Post. Los Angeles Times, September 9, 1990. Web. Accessed April 19, 2016.

Changing Minds

Imagine you support protecting national parks from too much tourism. Write a short essay trying to persuade your friend that Yellowstone should remain wild. Make sure you detail your opinion and your reasons for it. Include facts that support your reasons.

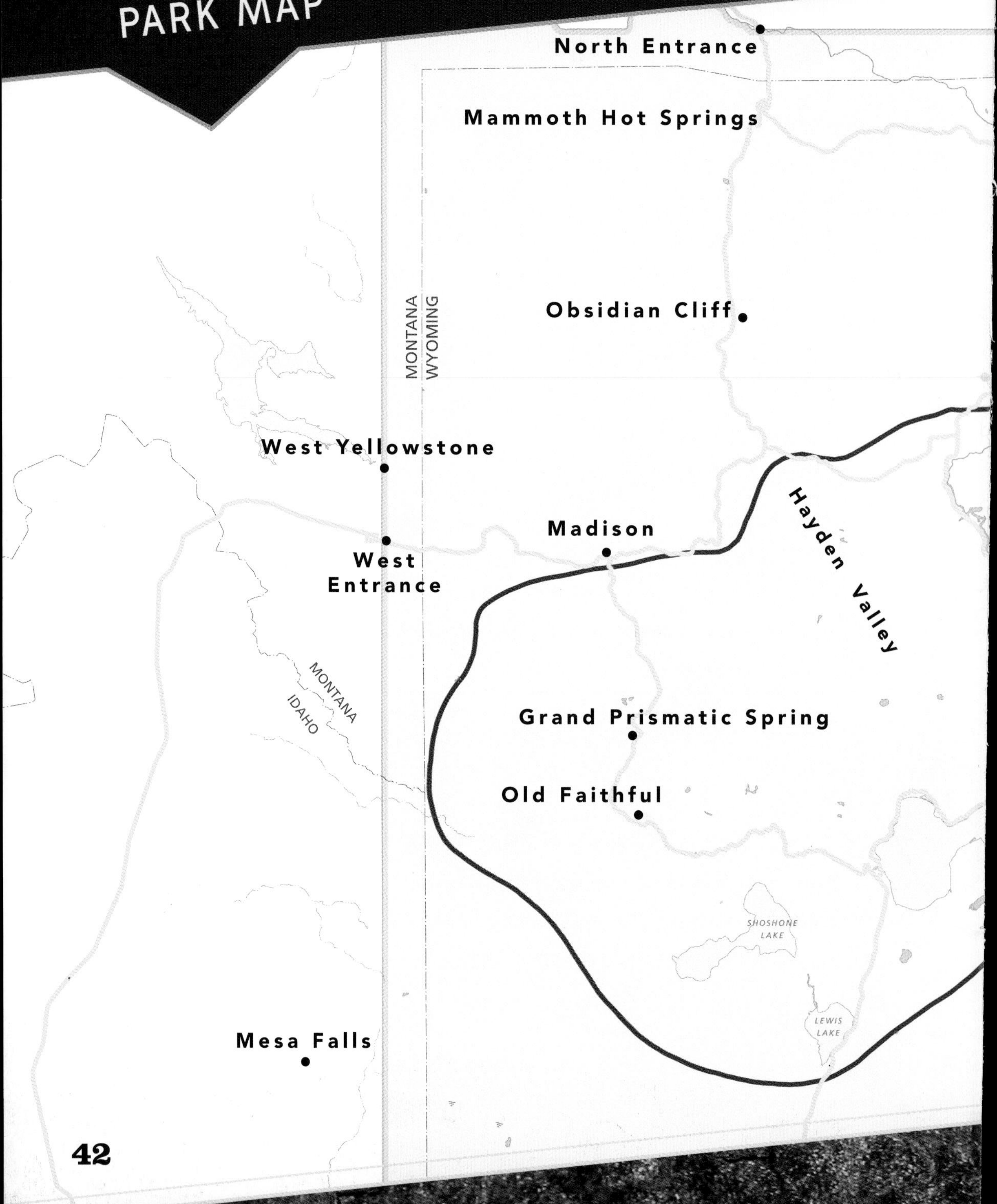

North Entrance

Mammoth Hot Springs

MONTANA
WYOMING

Obsidian Cliff

West Yellowstone

Madison

Hayden Valley

West
Entrance

MONTANA
IDAHO

Grand Prismatic Spring

Old Faithful

SHOSHONE
LAKE

LEWIS
LAKE

Mesa Falls

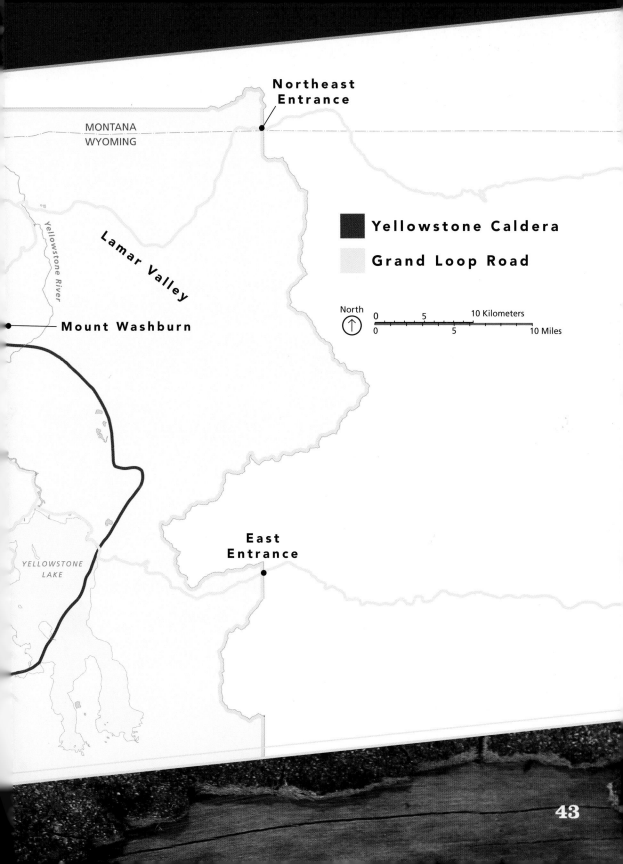

Northeast
Entrance

MONTANA
WYOMING

Lamar Valley

Yellowstone River

Mount Washburn

■ Yellowstone Caldera

□ Grand Loop Road

North

0   5   10 Kilometers
0   5   10 Miles

YELLOWSTONE
LAKE

East
Entrance

Tell the Tale

Chapter Five of this book discusses some of the research projects being conducted at Yellowstone National Park. Imagine you are a scientist doing a project at Yellowstone. Write 200 words describing your research. What type of scientist are you? Are you studying animals or plants? Or are you an archeologist? Describe what you have discovered during your time at Yellowstone.

Surprise Me

Chapter Two discusses the geology of Yellowstone National Park. After reading this book, what two or three facts about Yellowstone's geology did you find most surprising? Write a few sentences about each fact. Why did you find each fact surprising?

Dig Deeper

After reading this book, what questions do you still have about Yellowstone National Park? With an adult's help, find a few reliable sources that can help you answer your questions. Write a paragraph about what you learned.

Say What?

Studying a national park can mean learning a lot of new vocabulary. Find five words in this book you've never seen before. Use a dictionary to find out what they mean. Then write the meanings in your own words, and use each word in a new sentence.

GLOSSARY

biodiversity
many different plants and
animals living in an area

carcass
the dead body of an animal

climate change
a long-term change in
Earth's climate, including
temperature and weather
conditions

conservation
the protection of animals,
plants, and natural resources

ecosystem
a community of animals and
plants living together

lobby
to influence a government
decision

magma
melted rock beneath Earth's
surface

microbe
a tiny organism such as
bacteria that can only be
seen with a microscope

migrate
to move from place to place
depending on the time of
year

stagecoach
a four-wheeled closed vehicle
pulled by horses

LEARN MORE

Books

Hamilton, John. *Wyoming.* Minneapolis, MN: Abdo, 2017.

Kalman, Bobbie. *Yellowstone National Park.* New York: Crabtree, 2010.

Peabody, Erin. *A Weird and Wild Beauty: The Story of Yellowstone, the World's First National Park.* New York: Skyhorse, 2016.

Websites

To learn more about National Parks, visit **booklinks.abdopublishing.com**. These links are routinely monitored and updated to provide the most current information available.

Visit **mycorelibrary.com** for free additional tools for teachers and students.

INDEX

ABOUT THE AUTHOR

Cecilia Pinto McCarthy has written several nonfiction books for children. When she is not writing, she enjoys teaching ecology classes at a nature sanctuary. She lives with her family north of Boston, Massachusetts.